An **ILFORD** Colour Book of Flower Identification
General Editor: Peter Hunt

ROCK GARDEN PLANTS

by Will Ingwersen

Ebury Press
in association with George Rainbird

Other **ILFORD** Colour Books
in this Flower Identification Series

Available Now   **HOUSE PLANTS** by John Warren
CACTI AND OTHER SUCCULENTS
by Lieut.-General Sir Oliver Leese
HERBACEOUS PLANTS I by Peter Hunt
Later   **FLOWERING BULBS, CORMS AND TUBERS** by Frances Perry
FLOWERING SHRUBS AND TREES by S. A. Pearce
GREENHOUSE PLANTS by John Warren
HERBACEOUS PLANTS 2 by Peter Hunt
ANNUALS AND BIENNIALS by Roy Hay
ROSES by L. G. Turner

A Companion Series
Available Now   The **ILFORD** Colour Book of **FLOWER DECORATION** by Joan Groves
Later   **GARDENS IN COLOUR** by Peter Hunt

The colour photography is by James Adams, ARPS, T. Hamilton,
and Peter Hunt.
Thanks are due to the Director of the Royal Botanic Gardens, Kew,
the Royal Horticultural Society, Wisley and to many nursery owners
who allowed photographs to be taken.

First published 1965
© **ILFORD** Limited 1965

The colour photographs were produced on Ilfocolor film
and printed on Ilfocolor paper.
The end-paper illustrations, front and back, are of an *Erica* and are
reproduced from an Ilford X-ray photograph.
This book was designed and produced by George Rainbird Limited,
2 Hyde Park Place, London W.2,
and was printed in Great Britain by
Jarrold & Sons Limited, Norwich.

Will Ingwersen writes the text and captions
by arrangement with W. H. & L. Collingridge Ltd,
the proprietors of *Amateur Gardening*.

EDITOR'S PREFACE

Most gardeners like to be able to identify the plants which they grow or which they see growing in other gardens or in public parks and other places. But identification is not always easy, particularly when one considers how many different daisy-flowered plants are commonly grown, to mention but one family.

Conversely, when gardeners read about plants they like to see them illustrated, preferably in colour and especially if they are plants which are new to them. And, as Alice in Wonderland thought, 'What is the use of a book without pictures or conversations?' This series of Ilford Colour Books of Flower Identification supplies the pictures and, if not exactly conversations, then descriptions, all of which are designed to help readers to identify and grow over a thousand plants of many different kinds in their gardens or greenhouses or on their window-sills.

Many gardeners and flower lovers will wish to go on from here, using these books as a basis, and adding colour photographs of their own. Photographing flowers in colour is not difficult as Mr J. E. Downward FIBP shows on another page. From my own experience I can say that it is a rewarding pastime for it is very pleasant to be able to look back in the dead of winter to the garden as it was, to the flowers of spring and summer, to the colours of autumn, captured for ever in a colour photograph.

We are grateful for all the help we have received in the photographing of plants for this series, from, among many others, the Curator and his staff at the Royal Botanic Gardens, Kew, the Director and his staff at the Royal Horticultural Society's Gardens, Wisley, from many nurserymen and Parks Superintendents and from the authors of the various books. As General Editor of the series I must also say how impressed I have been with the assistance I have received from Ilford Limited, particularly from their staff at Cricklewood, and with the immense technical care which has been taken by all concerned at all stages of photography to ensure that the best results were obtained.

PETER HUNT

INTRODUCTION
What are Rock Garden Plants?

There is a quick answer to most questions and I suppose the easy reply to this one is 'any plant which will relish the rather specialized conditions provided by a properly constructed rock garden, and which will appear appropriate to its surroundings'. Like all quick responses, this one needs some qualification.

Rock garden plants are usually referred to as 'Alpines' and will be found so classified in nurserymen's catalogues and reference books. Controversy has always existed about the proper definition of an alpine plant. The wise gardener will not seek to define too exactly the plants which may be grown on a rock garden, or insist too strenuously upon a precise definition of an alpine plant. He will select from the multitudes of available plants those which most appeal to him, and which will appropriately adorn the miniature mountainscape which has been specially created for them to grow in.

It is fatally easy to place on a rock garden plants which will grow too large and be quite out of proportion to their surroundings. Mistakes are less likely to be made at the other end of the scale, for these are among the aristocrats of the plant world and possess qualities of character and dignity which are not dwarfed or rendered insignificant by the most majestic surroundings. The silvery, flower-strewn tufts of *Androsace helvetica* lose no jot or tittle of dignity because they grow on the crags of a mighty mountain whose towering peak pierces the clouds far above.

A novice is certain to make some mistakes in planting and these provide useful lessons, for we can all learn more from experience than from the spoken or written word.

Generally speaking plants of annual or biennial duration are not appropriate. Nearly all rock garden plants are perennials and, if pleased with their situation, will live, in ever-increasing beauty, for many years. One or two exceptions to the exclusion of annuals are to be found in dainty little *Ionopsidium acaule*, an inch-high plant with starry white and violet flowers, and such short-lived plants as *Papaver alpinum* and *Linaria alpina*, which will establish themselves contentedly, charmingly and harmlessly by means of self-sown seedlings. Any form of 'bedding out', using conventional annuals or biennials should be scrupulously avoided.

4

The temptation to fill blank spaces or to provide colour at awkward moments by using such colourful exotics as gazanias, mesembryanthemums or pelargoniums should be sternly resisted. On a well-planned and wisely planted rock garden they will be unnecessary, for it is not at all difficult to plant so that there is colour and interest, not only in the spring and early summer, but through the year and deep into the winter months.

Everyone who possesses a rock garden should also compile an *index expurgatorium*, consisting of the names of plants which, however appropriate they may seem, and however beautiful when in flower, are so invasive that it is unwise to plant them in any position that does not provide them with an almost unlimited area for expansion without harm to other plants. Among these should be included such plants as *Veronica filiformis* – a lovely but invasive fiend – all kinds of acaenas and cotulas, and *Sedum acre* and *S. album*. Under no circumstances whatever should that pretty green carpeter *Helxine solierolii* be admitted to any rock garden, and with it should also be excluded *Oxalis corniculata. Oxalis inops* and *O. chrysantha* are also invasive, but they can be kept in bounds and are so beautiful that they may be tolerated. Fortunately *O. chrysantha* is not fully hardy and even if its sheets of golden flowers have spread too widely, they will be drastically reduced by the first hard frost.

Membership of the Alpine Garden Society not only provides invaluable information through its excellent Quarterly Bulletin and its numerous regional exhibitions, but also keeps you in touch with other enthusiasts who have similar interests. Information as to the services it provides for members can be obtained from the Secretary, The Alpine Garden Society, 58, Denison House, Vauxhall Bridge Road, London, S.W.1.

Rock Garden Construction

Before constructing a rock garden the important decision must be made as to its situation. An obviously suitable site is not always available, but it is as well to have an ideal at which to aim, even though the position finally chosen may fall short of perfection in some details. The best of all sites is a gentle slope falling to the south or south-west, unshaded by trees or buildings and with good drainage beneath.

Excellent results may also be achieved in many other positions. It is important to avoid places which are overhung by trees, shaded by adjacent walls or buildings, or exposed to shrill draughts, which often flow through narrow passages between buildings. An essential consideration is the drainage. Alpine plants are amazingly tolerant of widely differing conditions of aspect, soil and climate, but none of them will endure sodden, sour soil. If the natural drainage is not good, then it must be made so before construction of the rock garden is started.

Should a sloping site be available it is a comparatively easy matter to drain away surplus water. It may not be so easy on a flat site, especially if the sub-soil is heavy and retentive of water. However, a deep sumphole filled with rubble, or any other coarse material, such as broken bricks, clinker, hard stone or even gravel, will dispose of all but exceptionally heavy rainfall and land drainage. Such a sump should be excavated approximately in the centre of the chosen area, and fed by narrow channels radiating to it from the circumference of the site, and similarly filled with some non-clogging material. This should provide adequate drainage.

With the position chosen, and prepared by being dug over and cleansed of all perennial weed roots, the time has come to decide what stone is to be used. A natural stone should be chosen if at all possible. Broken concrete lumps, clinker, or even old bricks are sometimes employed, but are never satisfactory. The only excuse for their use is an economic one, for, if there is no fairly local natural stone it may prove expensive to convey rocks from a considerable distance.

If a durable local stone exists it will be the least expensive, and it will also be in keeping with the surroundings. You may long for the handsome weather- and water-fretted limestone of northern counties, but unless you live within a reasonable distance of them, they are very expensive to transport.

A comparatively inexpensive and very suitable stone is to be found in Sussex sandstone. This is chemically neutral and may be used for both lime-loving and lime-hating plants. It is very porous and retains a lot of water. It weathers quickly and is a stone full of character, lending itself readily to the making of a rock garden which is pleasing to the eye, and which plants will like.

A ton of Sussex sandstone, delivered in pieces weighing from 28 lb to 1 cwt will provide enough stone to construct a small but practical rock garden. Very small pieces of stone are not of much use, with them it is not possible to build with dignity and substance. On the other hand, pieces weighing more than 1 cwt are not necessary in a small rock garden.

To describe the construction of a rock garden on paper is almost impossible. It is not so difficult to say what not to do. Do not place the stones in isolated splendour. They should join closely to each other so that several stones together give the appearance of one large boulder or outcrop of rock. Do not stand them on end. Bed the largest side into the ground and avoid isolated 'peaks'. Do not tilt them all ways, try to build so that all the stones tilt in the same direction and at approximately the same angle.

Before beginning the construction, try to visit a well-made rock garden, or study the stone you are using as it lies naturally before being quarried. This will give you a very definite idea of how to use it. Fiddle with a few stones on a trial run or two before making a start. Once you get the feel of the stone you will find the picture creating itself as you proceed. While it is most desirable that the finished result should look natural, and resemble a miniature mountainscape, it is also important to remember that the primary purpose of a rock garden is to grow plants.

Have a large heap of soil ready mixed before beginning to build. On a flat site, and with a ton of stone, about 3 cubic yards of soil compost will be needed. There is no need, in the early stages, to fuss with complicated recipes. These may be prepared for special plants later on. In the beginning be content with a standard mixture of loam, or good top-spit soil, leafsoil, or fine-grade granulated peat, and sharp sand or fine grit. If these ingredients are mixed in the proportions of 2 parts loam, 1 part peat and 1 part sand, this will provide a compost good enough for the majority of alpine plants. Under no circumstances use builder's sand. It must be a sharp, gritty material.

Most of the planting will be done when the rock garden has been built and has been left for a week or two for the soil in the pockets to settle, but crevice plants are more easily placed as the work proceeds, and a number of these should be at hand so that they can be inserted as the rocks are placed together. It is also useful to have a few quite bushy plants available so that, in places where a good join is not possible, a fault can be concealed by setting such a plant to hide it.

If a rock garden is not a possibility it may console you to know that alpine plants may be grown very successfully in other ways. They dwell very contentedly in between the stones of a dry wall, or in narrow chinks between paving stones, or failing any such crevices, most of them can be made quite at home in flat beds of very gritty soil, surfaced with an inch-thick layer of sharp grit or gravel. In fact, a number of enthusiastic gardeners, to whom the plants are of more importance than their surroundings, grow all their alpine plants without the aid of a rock garden.

Sinks and troughs of old stone, or receptacles of similar shape made from concrete, provide just the conditions needed to please many of the smaller, cushion-forming alpine plants. They find in such containers the right conditions of root confinement and sharp drainage needed to please them. Even a large, shallow seed-pan will provide space for a dozen or more small plants and even in such a limited area it is possible to contrive a tiny landscape by using small pieces of stone arranged in little outcrops.

A number of the more choice, high alpine plants demand rather more special conditions than can be provided in an ordinary rock garden, and if these are to be grown, a special scree area should be provided. This may be built in as the rock garden is constructed with little additional trouble or expense. All that is needed is a gently sloping area falling between outcrops of rock. The space allotted to the scree should be excavated to a depth of about 18 in. and the lower third filled with coarse rubble, over which upturned turves are placed. On top of this fill in with the standard compost, to which has been added an equal amount of pure grit, in the form of small stone chippings. A few solitary stones half buried in the surface of the scree will make it look more natural and will provide varying aspects on the several sides to please the taste of both sun-loving and sun-avoiding plants.

Except in the areas on the rock garden where larger plants are grown, it is a good plan to mulch the whole surface after planting with pure grit, to a depth of about half an inch. This retains moisture in the soil, and, if it is worked close in around the necks of the plants, helps to keep their collars dry and safe during the winter months.

General Cultivation

When the rock garden has been completed, and a period of two or three weeks allowed for settlement of the soil in the pockets, it will be time to consider what plants to choose. The choice is a wide one, for there are many hundreds of different species and varieties. The novice will do well to limit his first choice to plants which are easy to grow, leaving the more difficult kinds until greater experience makes success more likely.

In the beginning it is wise to stick to a few of the larger families, such as armerias, aubrietas, campanulas, dianthus, geraniums, helianthemums, phloxes, potentillas, saxifragas, sedums, sempervivums, thymes, veronicas, and so on. Choose from each family a few varieties. As a guide to a collection of fifty easy plants for a beginner I would suggest the following:

Armeria maritima laucheana and *A. maritima* 'Vindictive'.

Aubrieta. Half a dozen chosen from a catalogue to give a variety of colours. Select named kinds and not seedlings sold as a mixture.

Campanula carpatica, C. cochlearifolia and *C. portenschlagiana.*

Dianthus arvernensis, D. caesius and *D. deltoides.*

Geranium sanguineum lancastriense, G. renardii and *G. subcaulescens.*

Helianthemum 'Firedragon', *H.* 'Jubilee', *H.* 'Mrs Earle', *H.* 'The Bride' and *H.* 'Watergate Rose'.

Phlox subulata 'G. F. Wilson', *P. subulata* 'Model', *P. subulata* 'Oakington Blue Eyes' and *P. subulata* 'Temiscaming'.

Potentilla alpestris, P. aurea plena, P. megalantha and *P. tonguei.*

Saxifraga aizoon lutea, S. aizoon rosea, S. apiculata, S. 'Four Winds' and *S. lingulata.*

Sedum cauticola, S. ewersii, S. hybridum, S. lydium, S. pulchellum (in a cool position, all other sedums like hot, dry places) and *S.* 'Schorbusser Blut'.

Sempervivum arachnoideum, S. heufellii, S. montanum, S. ornatum, and *S. tectorum calcareum.*

Thymus serpyllum, three forms chosen for the colour of their flowers and *T.* 'Silver Queen'.

Veronica cataractae, V. pageana, V. pectinata rosea, V. prostrata, V. prostrata alba, and *V. prostrata rosea.*

That is actually more than fifty, for good measure, and will form a good nucleus from which to expand.

Alpines like to be planted firmly, in soil which is not a loose bed of compost. This is why it is better to delay planting until the soil has settled. Nearly all alpine plants are grown in pots and will be received with a firm root ball. If this is hard it should be gently loosened with the fingers before planting. Then make a hole deep enough to contain all the roots without doubling them up, set the plant so that its neck, or collar, is just level with the surface of the soil, fill around with compost and press gently but very firmly. Plants which grow in the form of a tight, compact cushion of rosettes like to be wedged in tightly with small, flattish pieces of stone. These can be placed after planting, and pushed right in under the cushion so that the pad of rosettes rests on a hard surface of stone.

For all the plants suggested above and for a great many others of the easier kinds, the standard compost is quite suitable. It is necessary, however, to know whether the plants being used are lovers or haters of lime. If the soil you are using is alkaline, that is, containing lime in some form, certain plants must be avoided, or given separate pockets of lime-free soil. A few to which this reservation applies are:

Lithospermum 'Heavenly Blue' and *L.* 'Grace Ward', all the autumn flowering Asiatic gentians such as *Gentiana sino-ornata, G. macaulayi* etc., all heathers with the exception of *Erica carnea,* which will grow in chalky soil, all rhododendrons, and, in fact, almost all plants which belong to the natural order *Ericaceae*. Nearly all alpine plant catalogues give warning of plants which dislike lime. The lime-lovers will grow quite well in lime-free soil.

Alpines which have leaves densely felted with soft hairs may appreciate some winter protection against wet. They are probably perfectly hardy and even severe cold will not affect them, but in nature they are accustomed to be buried safely beneath a snow-covering during the winter, which keeps them dry. All that is needed is a pane of glass secured in some way so that overhead moisture is thrown off. Even this slight precaution is unnecessary for the plants so far recommended.

The propagation of alpine plants is usually effected by raising them from seed, or by taking cuttings when soft growth tips are available. Seeds of hybrids will not come true and such plants as these must be increased by cuttings. Named varieties of aubrieta, helianthemum and phlox will not breed true from seed, but seeds may confidently be sown of all species and many varieties. Save the seed as soon as it is ripe and, as far as all members of the primula and ranunculus family are concerned, sow it as soon as possible. Most other seeds may be kept in a cool, dry place and sown in February.

Sow in pans or boxes, on to a gritty compost. Fine seeds can be sown direct on to a final layer of fine grit without any additional covering. Larger seeds should have fine soil sifted over them so that they are just covered. Cover the receptacles, after sowing and soaking, with glass and brown paper and exclude light until they germinate.

Cuttings are made from non-flowering soft tips, an inch or two in length, removing the lower leaves from the stem and cutting immediately below a leaf-joint with a very sharp knife. Insert the cuttings into pure sand, or very sandy soil, in pans, pots or boxes, and keep in a close frame until they root, shading them against full sunlight and watering when necessary to keep them just moist.

Of many alpine plants it will be found possible to remove small rooted portions in spring or autumn. These may be potted separately and grown on into sturdy young plants. Very often more rapid propagation is possible by lifting a mature plant and carefully dividing it into small portions each having some root. These, if potted and kept in a close frame for a few days will provide adult plants more quickly than either seeds or cuttings.

Make certain that all plants are clearly labelled, using labels which have some permanence. Metal labels of some kind, written on with a recommended ink, are the best and endure much longer than any wooden label inscribed in pencil. Nothing is easier, or more annoying, than to lose the name of a plant and regular attention should be given to the rock garden to ensure that the labels are readable.

The following lists will serve as a guide for a particular situation.

Plants for full sun

Aethionema, all kinds
Alyssum, all kinds
Anagallis linifolia
Anaphalis triplinervis
Androsace, all kinds
Anemone pulsatilla
Antennaria dioica, and all varieties
Aquilegia, all kinds
Arabis albida, all varieties
Armeria, all kinds
Aster purdomii
Aubrieta, all kinds
Calamintha alpina
Campanula, all kinds
Centaurium scilloides
Cheiranthus, all kinds
Crocus, all kinds
Cyananthus microphyllus (integer)
Daphne cneorum
Dryas octopetala
Edraianthus pumilio
Erica carnea
Erigeron mucronatus
Erinus alpinus, all varieties
Gentiana acaulis
Gentiana septemfida
Geranium 'Ballerina'
Geum montanum
Gypsophila fratensis
Halimiocistus sahucii
Helianthemum nummularium, all varieties
Hypericum, all kinds

Iberis sempervirens 'Snowflake'
Ipheion uniflorum
Iris reticulata, all varieties
Leontopodium alpinum
Lewisia, all kinds
Linum, all kinds
Lithospermum diffusum 'Grace Ward'
Lotus corniculatus flore-pleno
Nierembergia repens (rivularis)
Oenothera missouriensis
Origanum vulgare aureum
Penstemon scouleri
Phlox subulata, all varieties
Platycodon grandiflorum mariesii
Potentilla ambigua
Potentilla fruticosa, all varieties
Potentilla tonguei
Ranunculus ficaria aurantiaca
Rhodohypoxis baurei
Saponaria ocymoides
Saxifraga apiculata
Saxifraga longifolia 'Tumbling Waters'
Scilla sibirica
Scilla tubergeniana
Scutellaria baicalensis
Sedum, all kinds except *S. pulchellum*
Sempervivum, all kinds
Silene schafta
Tulipa, all kinds
Veronica prostrata, all varieties
Viola cornuta alba
Viola gracilis major

Plants for shade

Anagallis tenella
Anemone nemorosa, all varieties
Astilbe chinensis pumila
Cornus canadensis
Cyclamen europaeum
Cyclamen neapolitanum
Cyclamen repandum
Daphne blagayana
Dicentra formosa
Erythronium dens-canis
Haberleas
Hacquetia epipactis
Houstonia caerulea

Mentha requienii
Mertensia virginica
Mitchella repens
Omphalodes verna
Oxalis acetosella rosea
Parochetus communis
Pulmonarias, all kinds
Ramonda myconii
Roscoea humeana
Saxifraga umbrosa, all varieties
Shortia uniflora
Tiarella cordifolia
Waldsteinia ternata

Plants for poor conditions

Alyssum saxatile, all varieties
Anaphalis triplinervis

Antennaria, all kinds
Antirrhinum asarina

Arabis albida, all varieties
Aubrieta. all kinds
Cheiranthus cheiri 'Harpur Crewe'
Erigeron mucronatus
Gypsophila fratensis, all varieties
Helianthemum nummularium, all varieties
Iberis sempervirens 'Snowflake'
Nierembergia repens (*rivularis*)
Polygonum vaccinifolium

Potentilla fruticosa, all varieties
Potentilla tonguei
Ranunculus ficaria, all varieties
Saponaria ocymoides
Saxifraga umbrosa, all varieties
Sedums, all varieties
Sempervivum, all varieties
Silene schafta
Waldsteinia ternata

The fact that plants are included in the above list does not necessarily imply that they MUST have poor soil, but merely indicates that they will grow in conditions too impoverished to please other plants.

Plants for walls

Aethionema, all kinds
Alyssum, all kinds
Androsace lanuginosa leichtlinii
Androsace primuloides
Antirrhinum asarina
Arabis, all kinds
Aubrieta, all kinds
Calamintha alpina
Campanula, all kinds other than border
  varieties
Cheiranthus cheiri 'Harpur Crewe'
Dryas octopetala
Erigeron mucronatus
Erinus alpinus, all varieties
Gypsophila fratensis, all varieties
Helianthemum nummularium, all varieties

Hypericum rhodopaeum
Iberis sempervirens 'Snowflake'
Lewisia howellii
Lithospermum diffusum 'Grace Ward'
Lotus corniculatus flore-pleno
Penstemon scouleri
Phlox subulata, all varieties
Polygonum vaccinifolium
Ramonda myconii
Saponaria ocymoides
Saxifraga longifolia 'Tumbling Waters'
Sempervivum, all kinds
Silene schafta
Veronica prostrata all varieties
Waldsteinia ternata

Plants for sink gardens

Aethionema 'Warley Rose'
Alyssum wulfenianum
Anacyclus depressus
Androsace sarmentosa, all varieties
Antennaria dioica rosea
Arabis, cushion-forming species
Arenaria tetraquetra
Armeria caespitosa
Asperula suberosa
Bellium minutum
Campanula cochlearifolia (*pusilla*)
Cotyledon chrysantha
Crassula sediformis
Cyclamen coum
Dianthus neglectus (no lime)
Erinus alpinus, all varieties

Erodium chamaedrioides roseum
Genista pilosa procumbens
Geranium farreri
Gypsophila fratensis
Helichrysum milfordae
Iris cristata lacustris
Linaria alpina
Lychnis alpina
Minuartia verna
Morisia monanthos (*hypogaea*)
Phlox douglasii, all varieties
Primula minima
Ranunculus crenatus
Saxifraga, all 'Kabschia' varieties
Sedum lydium

Photographing Plants in Colour

BY J. E. DOWNWARD FIBP

How often one hears from a keen gardener showing you round his garden, 'You should see it in the spring when it is alive with colour' or 'It is brilliant in the autumn, when the foliage colours'. One is never there at the right time. This is a joke amongst gardeners used by the late Ruth Draper, to great advantage, in one of her humorous monologues. These incredulous stories can now be substantiated by the camera and the use of the colour films which are available today.

There are Ilford colour films for prints and slides. When mounted in an album, prints will be a source of great pleasure to the gardener photographer and his friends throughout the year, and especially when work outside is impossible owing to unsuitable weather conditions.

With a 35 mm camera slides can be made which, when projected on a screen in a darkened room, will verify stories of past glories in the garden and even give the owner another thrill, perhaps in the depth of winter when the display outside is far from pleasing.

Photographing growing plants in the garden presents little difficulty regarding apparatus, but when taking 'close up' pictures of flowers it is particularly necessary to pay attention to the accuracy of focusing the subject. Cameras of the reflex type or those which incorporate a range finder are a great help. When relying on the scale on the camera it is wise to measure the distance from lens to subject and check that it is the same. It may be found that the focusing scale does not allow one to take really close up photographs, as it is not possible to focus nearer than 2 or 3 ft. Supplementary lenses or extension tubes may be purchased to overcome this problem, and a photographic dealer will advise and supply these to suit the camera. It will then be possible to make portraits of individual blooms or even certain parts of a flower.

Some support for the camera, such as a tripod, is essential for close up photography especially when the lighting is less brilliant and longer exposures are necessary.

Accurate exposure is one of the vital factors in colour photography, and the photo-electric exposure meter provides the best method of calculation. Study the maker's instructions and understand the working of the meter before making an exposure. It is very useful to enter all errors of exposure in a log book so that they may be corrected when taking further pictures.

Slides which are thin and weak in colour are over exposed and a smaller aperture must be used in the future. If the slides are dense and the colours too dark they are under exposed and a larger aperture will then have to be used. A photo-electric exposure meter, if used as instructed, should give correct exposure, but shutter speeds vary, so do lenses, which may account for any variation in the results. The meter may not have been held correctly when taking the reading; it is a common fault to tilt the meter upwards and so admit reflected light from the sky, which may not even appear in the picture. The printed instructions, which are packed with the film, give helpful suggestions for exposure under various lighting conditions, and even without an exposure meter it is possible to produce good results. With a little practice and references to one's log book it is possible to become very experienced in judging exposure, but a meter makes the calculation much easier.

When the daylight is not very brilliant blue flash bulbs may be used, for colour photography, with Daylight colour film, and if two or three bulbs are used in reflectors a soft even lighting will be produced which is ideal for flowers. The leaflet with the bulbs will give you a speed index for various films and a corresponding Guide Number for each speed. This Guide No. is used to decide what lens aperture or f/number is necessary when the flash bulb is held at certain distances away from the subject. Suppose a PF1 Blue bulb is being used and the Guide No. on the leaflet is 65 for the film in the camera. Then if the flash bulb is held 10 ft away from the flower being taken, 10 should be divided into 65; the answer is 6·5 and hence the stop to use, in this case, is f6·5. However, if it is found that a smaller aperture is needed to obtain a sharp picture, divide the aperture f/No. into the Guide No. and the answer will be the distance the flash bulb should be from the subject. For example, again with the above Guide No. of 65, it may be decided that an aperture of f16 is necessary, 16 divided into 65 gives an answer of about 4 and so the distance of the flash bulb from the subject should be 4 ft.

Assuming the shutter is correctly synchronized, shutter speed is not important as long as it covers the duration of the flash, which actually makes the exposure; 1/30th or 1/50th second should be satisfactory. If the shutter is not synchronized it is possible to use 'Open Flash', that is, use a B speed setting, press the shutter, fire the flash bulb while the shutter is open and then close it as quickly as possible. Owing to the length of exposure, which may be about one second, this method is only possible in poor light and when there is no breeze to move the flowers and the camera is absolutely steady.

It is very worth while making oneself as expert as possible in the working of the camera and the technique of taking a photograph, so that more time may then be spent on the composition of the picture.

Care in the choice of background to make the subject stand out, for example; a movement of view-point will often achieve this, by bringing into the picture some other plant or shrub which makes the subject more prominent. The height of the camera may contribute to making the picture more dramatic, and in some instances give an added beauty to a flower when viewed from an unfamiliar angle. Study the position of the subject, walk round it, and choose the view-point carefully before taking the photograph.

Index of Common Names

1

Adonis brevistyla (*Ranunculaceae*)

A deciduous, perennial plant easily grown in well-drained soil and an open, sunny position. The soft green leaves are deeply cut and almost fern-like in appearance. The flowers are produced in the spring on branching stems which vary in height from 6 in. when the plant begins flowering to 12 in. at maturity. The petals of the inch-wide flowers are white on the upper side and blue beneath. Propagate by division as soon as growth commences in the early spring, or by sowing the seeds, which should be sown as soon as they detach easily from the seedhead and while still green. *Adonis davidii* is a synonym.

2

Aethionema 'Warley Rose' (*Cruciferae*)

An invaluable, summer-flowering dwarf shrub for warm, sunny places in the rock garden, needing only well-drained soil and the avoidance of very wet winter conditions. Woody stems clothed with tiny green leaves and innumerable heads of deep rose-pink flowers. It has all the appearance, when in flower, of a small daphne, and may well be used in place of these more temperamental plants in gardens where they do not flourish, although it lacks the characteristic fragrance of daphne. At maturity plants are approximately 6 to 9 in. tall. Do not disturb when once established. Seed is not produced and the plant must be propagated from cuttings: soft tips in early spring or after flowering, or inch-long side-shoots removed with a small heel of older wood.

1

2

3

4

3

Alyssum saxatile (*Cruciferae*) **Gold Dust**

This is the type species of a number of valuable, sun-loving rock-garden plants. Grow in soil which is poor rather than rich, and cut the plants back hard after flowering. Propagate by spring and summer cuttings. Seedlings may be raised but do not usually breed true to the plant from which they were taken. The innumerable clusters of golden flowers are produced in early spring on 9 to 12 in. stems. Good named varieties are: *Alyssum saxatile* 'Dudley Neville', buff-yellow, *citrinum*, soft lemon-yellow, and *compactum*, a particularly dwarf form of the type.

4

Amaracus pulcher (Origanum) (*Labiatae*) **Marjoram**

The marjorams are a race of upstanding herbaceous plants, many having great beauty. They like warm, sunny positions and appreciate protection from east winds. Their soil should be sharply drained and of good substance. Good loam, with added leafsoil or peat, and sharp sand or grit is an excellent compost. *Amaracus pulcher* comes from the Levant and carries its tiny flowers between showy pink bracts in nodding, hop-like heads on stems of about 12 in. in high summer. Propagate by cuttings.

5

Anagallis linifolia (Primulaceae)

Our native, annual Scarlet Pimpernel is an anagallis, and, beloved though it is, has no garden value. Several of the exotic species, however, are extremely decorative, and few more so than *Anagallis linifolia*, which is native to warm Mediterranean regions. It is a perennial, though sometimes short-lived in cultivation. Its spreading, prostrate stems carry innumerable wide-open deep blue flowers throughout the summer months. Grow it in light soil and full sun, and save some seeds or strike a few cuttings each year in case it does not survive the winter.

6

Anaphalis triplinervis (Compositae)

A useful and decorative plant which can be grown in sun or dry shade. It is a little too tall for a small rock garden but is valuable in larger ones or in the front of a flower border. The 12 to 15 in. stems are covered with silver hairs and the leaves are equally silvery. The bunched heads of white flowers last for a long time, their virtue resting in the papery bracts which surround the inconspicuous flowers. They may be cut and dried for winter use. Any well-drained soil is suitable, but richly manured ground is best avoided as this produces unduly tall stems and too much leaf at the expense of flower. Propagate by division in spring or autumn and by seed. A similar, but dwarfer species, rather more suitable for rock gardens, is *Anaphalis nubigena*.

5

6

7

8

7

Androsace primuloides (*Primulaceae*) **Rock Jasmine**

This androsace is one of the more easy kinds and flourishes in gritty soil and a sunny position. Rosettes of glossy leaves form a dense mat, above which rise 4 in. stems carrying heads of pink flowers in the spring. It much resembles the well-known *Androsace sarmentosa*, but lacks the pelt of grey hairs. Young rosettes are carried on short stems and may be detached and rooted as cuttings, or removed with roots already formed in mid-summer. Seed is produced and germinates readily if sown as soon as it is ripe.

8

Androsace sarmentosa yunnanensis (*Primulaceae*) **Rock Jasmine**

Some species of androsace are difficult to grow and are best left to skilled growers who can accommodate them in alpine houses. This is an excellent plant for those who prefer more easily pleased plants. Its grey-green rosettes of small, hairy leaves form dense carpets and are concealed beneath a wealth of bright pink flowers in rounded heads on 6 in. stems during the spring. Grow in very gritty soil and full sun. Propagate by lifting rooted rosettes in spring or autumn. In very wet winters a trifle of protection from rain is appreciated, but not essential.

9

Anemone nemorosa allenii (*Ranunculaceae*) **Windflower**

Deeply though we love the wild wood anemone of copse and spinney it is not a plant commonly grown in gardens, where its place is taken by several of its varieties. A notable beauty is this particular form, which is similar in leaf and stature to our native plant, but has larger flowers, of soft powder blue. It should be grown in rather heavy soil, which is nevertheless well drained, and either in light shade or in a cool, north aspect. The place where it is growing should be well marked as it is deciduous, dying down after flowering in the spring. It can be increased by lifting and dividing old clumps very early in the year, even before the leaves appear above ground.

10

Anemone pulsatilla (*Ranunculaceae*) **Pasque Flower**

A valuable and variable harbinger of spring. Loves soil rich in lime and full sun. Old plants should never be disturbed. Plant young, well-rooted seedlings and leave severely alone. In its smallest and neatest form it is a rare native of Britain and, if found, should be admired but not collected. Across the English Channel, in Brittany and Normandy, the plant grows in profusion on the chalk downs and in a multiplicity of colour forms. From tufts of deeply divided, fern-like leaves rise erect stems carrying large flowers, which, according to the particular variety, may be pale or deep purple, pink, soft or deep red. There is one rare form from the Caucasus mountains with primrose-yellow flowers. Propagate by seeds, which should be sown in sandy soil soon after they are ripe, by inserting them closely together, and upright, spearing them into the soil by holding their long awns.

9

10

11

12

11

Antennaria dioica 'Nyewoods' (*Compositae*)

A creeping, slightly invasive but beautiful little plant. It is very suitable for creating ground cover in sunny parts of the rock garden, beneath which to plant small alpine bulbs such as the dwarf kinds of narcissus, scilla, muscari, etc. Silver-grey leaves in small rosettes form a close carpet and the tufts of tiny pink flowers are carried on 3 in. stems in spring and early summer. Rich soil should be avoided as this encourages rampant growth. It likes poor, gritty compost. It is also an excellent plant for growing in the crevices between paving stones. Propagate by division at almost any time of the year.

12

Antirrhinum asarina (*Scrophulariaceae*) **Snapdragon**

This is a handsome creeping snapdragon from Southern Europe. It loves to grow so that it can scramble downwards from narrow ledges and chinks between large stones and can also be used to great advantage in a wall. The hoary leaves clothe long, trailing stems and from the leaf axils spring solitary, large, cream-white flowers with a yellow lip. It is not at all particular about soil as long as the drainage is good, and can be increased both by seeds and by rooting the soft tips of young shoots as cuttings.

13

Aquilegia flabellata alba (Ranunculaceae) **Columbine**

Aquilegias are notoriously amoral plants which hybridize with great freedom and seldom come true from seed. This is one of the exceptions and may be relied upon to reproduce itself faithfully by seed, which is one of the only methods of propagation as it does not divide readily. Rather waxy, wide-lobed, grey-green leaves form a handsome foil for the large, ivory-white flowers which are carried on stiff, erect stems about 9 to 12 in. tall. It is by no means fussy about soil or position and will grow well in any sharply drained compost and in full sun.

14

Arabis albida (Cruciferae)

Arabis albida itself is seldom grown, its place being more worthily occupied by one or other of the handsome named varieties. Of these one of the most popular is the form with large, fully double snow-white flowers named *Arabis albida flore-pleno*. There is a good form with rose-red single flowers named *A. albida coccinea* and another with gold and silver variegated foliage and single white flowers. Grow them all in soil which is sharply drained and not too rich. They are magnificent wall plants and all flower in the early spring, making good company for aubrietas and alyssums.

13

14

15

16

15

Armeria caespitosa rubra (*Plumbaginaceae*) **Thrift**

This cushion-forming tiny Spanish thrift is a very good plant to grow in a gritty scree in full sun. The common thrifts grow well in any ordinary soil but this alpine form likes a sparser diet. The narrow, dark green leaves are tightly gathered into small tufts which are again assembled into hard, close tuffets making rounded, dark green pin-cushions on the ground. In the spring and early summer these are studded with many heads of deep pink flowers, either stemless, or raised only just above the foliage. As it does not come entirely true from seed, propagation is best by division of old plants, or by pulling a tuft to pieces in the spring and inserting each tiny cluster of 'rosettes' as a cutting, with a long portion of the old stem to act as a leg.

16

Aster purdomii (*Compositae*)

One of the rather taller alpine asters, and a showy, easily grown and useful plant for May and June flowering. It should not be planted too near to small plants as it is capable of growing into a vigorous clump, with strong leaves and stems nearly a foot in height, carrying large, violet-blue aster flowers with golden centres. It can be propagated easily either by dividing an old plant in spring or autumn, or by saving and sowing the seeds which it produces plentifully. The correct name is *Aster flaccidus*.

17

Astilbe chinensis pumila (*Saxifragaceae*)

The type plant comes from China and will grow to a height of more than 2 ft. This pygmy variety is seldom more than 12 in. tall and flowers in the late summer, at a time when its rich colour is invaluable on the rock garden. It should be given a cool position in soil which holds moisture, where it will make bold tufts of deeply divided leaves, surmounted by plumy spikes of small, mulberry-red flowers. Increase by division in spring or late autumn.

18

Aubrieta 'Godstone' (*Cruciferae*) **Rock Cress**

The named garden forms of aubrieta which make such a major contri-bution to spring colour in the rock garden are all derived from the species *Aubrieta deltoides*, a plant which has little if any garden value. The glowing violet-purple flowers of 'Godstone' make it one of the most popular among the numerous modern varieties. Aubrietas love sunshine and lime. They are wonderful plants with which to clothe a wall, or for placing so that they can hang downwards from crevices or over the edges of large stones in the rock garden. After flowering they should be cut back hard and top-dressed with good soil containing bonemeal. Propagate the named kinds by cuttings or division. They do not come true from seed.

17 19

18 20

19

Calamintha alpina (*Labiatae*)

A neat little alpine plant which, though not especially showy, flowers
for a long period and wins the affection of all who grow it. It flourishes
in any well-drained soil and in sun or light shade. The wiry, leafy stems
grow into little bushes about 6 in. high and carry many whorls of small
purple flowers. It is a good plant to use in a small alpine lawn or meadow
and delights in close association with other plants of similar habit,
such as the alpine toadflax, *Linaria alpina*, or small alpine hypericums.
Propagate by seed or by cuttings of soft tips.

20

Campanula carpatica 'Blue Moonlight' (*Campanulaceae*)
Bellflower

Campanulas are invaluable for providing late summer colour in the
rock garden, and few can equal the forms of *Campanula carpatica* when
it comes to making a generous display of large, brightly coloured
flowers. They are robust plants, needing a fair amount of space – they
should be planted at least 12 in. apart – and given good, well-drained
soil and a sunny position. The named varieties of *C. carpatica*, such as
this one, should be increased by cuttings or division. Seed will produce
a mixture of differing colour and habit. The flowers of 'Blue Moonlight'
are carried on 9 in. stems and are of a delicate blue shade.

21

Campanula carpatica turbinata 'Jewel' (*Campanulaceae*)
Bellflower

This form of *Campanula carpatica* is a gem for an open, sunny position
in gritty soil. It grows in the form of tidy tufts of leaves, over which, on
short stems, are carried so many wide-open purple-blue flowers that
the whole plant is obscured by the blossoms in June and July. It will
not come true from seed, though interesting variations may confidently
be expected, and should be increased by division or carefully made
cuttings of young, non-flowering shoots.

22

Centaurium scilloides (*Gentianaceae*)

A dainty cousin of the gentians which should be grown in gritty soil
which is rich in humus and capable of retaining moisture during
drought. It likes a position sheltered from the hottest sunshine, but not
in dense shade. The tiny, rounded green leaves make neat mats at
ground level and the tubular pink flowers are carried on 3 in. stems in
the spring. Propagate by division, cuttings and seed. It is perennial
but not very long-lived, and young plants should be grown on every
year or two to replace those which finally flower themselves to death.
Synonyms are *Erythraea massonii* and *E. diffusa*.

21

22

23

24

23

Cheiranthus cheiri 'Moonlight' (*Cruciferae*) **Wallflower**

There are several perennial wallflowers, forms and hybrids of *Cheiranthus cheiri*, which are excellent rock-garden plants. They should be grown in well-drained soil containing ample humus, and in full sun. The large flowers of 'Moonlight' are soft yellow in colour and gathered in compact heads on 9 to 12 in. stems. It flowers over a prolonged period in early summer. Propagate by cuttings only, made from soft tips, or firmer shoots taken with a heel of older wood.

24

Chrysogonum virginianum (*Compositae*)

This is a decorative and useful, and rather neglected plant. It grows with the greatest good nature in any soil which is not too dry, and will flourish in sun or light shade. The semi-creeping stems are adorned with rather rough, pointed leaves and carry many star-shaped rich yellow flowers from late spring until late summer. It sometimes produces seed from which it can be propagated, but it is more usually increased by division or by cuttings. It is a useful ground coverer between other, taller plants in the rock garden and is also effective when allowed to sprawl over low stones by a pathside.

25

Cornus canadensis (*Cornaceae*) **Creeping Dogwood**

A beautiful, low-growing woody plant which prefers lime-free soil and should be grown in light shade or with a cool north aspect. It spreads by means of underground stems and forms a dense carpet of erect, woody stems about 6 in. high, crowned with oval green leaves. The large, white, flower-like bracts appear in June and July and are often followed by red berries. An old plant can be lifted during the winter and divided if additional plants are required. It is a perfect ground coverer to use beneath and between taller shrubs and trees and is also very happy when allowed to wander at will through the walls and beds of a peat garden, where it serves a useful as well as a decorative purpose by preventing erosion of the peat walls.

26

Crocus chrysanthus 'Cream Beauty' (*Iridaceae*)

The species *Crocus chrysanthus* comes from Greece and Asia Minor and is best known in gardens in the form of the many beautiful seedling varieties which have been raised and named. It is a spring-flowering crocus, often producing its flowers during February. The particular variety illustrated here is a handsome flower of cream, with dainty featherings on the flower segments. Plant the corms in late summer or early autumn, in groups, spacing them about 3 in. apart and not more than 2 in. deep, in light, well-drained soil and a sunny spot.

25

26

27

28

27

Crocus susianus 'Cloth of Gold' (*Iridaceae*)

This is another spring-flowering crocus which presents the brilliant carpet of its brilliant gold flowers to every ray of February sunshine. It is a useful crocus to use for naturalizing in broad drifts in sunny places and fairly light soil. It has the same fatal attraction for birds that most yellow spring crocuses have and often has to be protected with a few strands of black cotton.

28

Cyananthus microphyllus (*Campanulaceae*)

An aristocratic cousin of the campanulas and worthy of the special position it prefers, in very gritty soil and a sunny, but not arid position. It is a splendid scree plant. The wiry stems radiate from a stout root to form a close pattern flat on the ground, and every leaf-clad stem ends in a large, deep blue flower centred by a fluff of deeper blue stamens. It is deciduous, and cuttings made from the first soft shoots, before buds are developed, will root. It can also be raised from the seeds it produces freely. *Cyananthus integer* is another name for this plant.

29

Cyclamen neapolitanum album (Primulaceae)

Hardy cyclamen should be planted in every rock garden. This is the white form of the pink-flowered species which begins to produce its exquisitely shaped flowers in August. Corms should be planted as growing plants; they are more likely to establish and colonize than dried corms long stored as dry bulbs. Set the corms 2 in. beneath the soil and 4 or 5 in. apart in a cool or shaded corner, in soil rich in humus. If the pink and the white variety are planted together a delightful picture is created. Propagation is by seed, sown as soon as possible after ripening–even so it may be a long time germinating.

30

Daphne cneorum (Thymeliaceae) **Garland Flower**

There is no more beautiful dwarf shrub for the rock garden than this gloriously fragrant daphne. Most daphnes are inclined to be temperamental and care should be taken to plant it well, in good, deep loam soil and in an open position. As time passes its woody stems are apt to become leafless and when this happens peaty soil should be heaped up in the centre of the plant, covering the bare stems to the point where leaves begin. About 12 in. in height, *Daphne cneorum* makes a neat, evergreen bush and every shoot ends in a cluster of deep pink flowers whose fragrance fills the air for yards around in early summer. Propagate by cuttings or rooted layers.

29

30

31

32

31

Dicentra formosa (Papaveraceae) **Locket Flower**

Here is a good plant for a semi-shaded place in any good, well-drained soil. Its leaves are ferny and graceful and above them, on 15 in. stems, hang innumerable lovely, locket-shaped pink flowers in May. It appreciates generous treatment and a top-dressing of new soil each spring, just as new growth begins to appear above the ground after its period of winter dormancy. Old plants may be lifted in autumn or spring and divided into rooted pieces for replanting. Spring is preferable unless it can be done while the soil is still warm in the early autumn.

32

Dryas octopetala (Rosaceae) **Mountain Avens**

A rare British native, which should be respected when encountered and left untouched. It is common in the Alps, and plants are always obtainable from nurserymen who grow alpine plants. It is a prostrate shrub, with trailing, woody stems densely clothed with small, dark green, rather leathery oak-shaped leaves. The large, 8-petalled flowers are like those of a pure white dog-rose and are carried effectively above the sombre foliage on short stems in spring and off and on during the summer. Any well-drained soil and a sunny place please it well. Propagate by seeds, cuttings, or by detaching rooted stems and potting them until established.

33

Edraianthus pumilio (*Campanulaceae*)

This is a choice little alpine plant best suited in a sunny, gritty scree with very sharp drainage and not too much rich soil. It grows into tidy little pincushions of silver, narrow leaves and bears lavender bell flowers on short stems in the spring and early summer. It is seldom more than 2 in. high and should be planted near at hand so that its beauty can be readily appreciated. Save the seeds, noting that they escape immediately they are ripe so that the pods must be handled very carefully. It makes a deep tap-root and does not relish being dug up and divided, and the rooting of its tiny cuttings is a highly skilled operation.

34

Eranthis cilicica (*Ranunculaceae*) **Winter Aconite**

The plant commonly known as Winter Aconite is *Eranthis hyemalis*. The plant illustrated is another species, slightly taller growing and not quite so ready to colonize. It should be grown in well-drained soil, and loves lime. Plant the tubers in late summer or early autumn and do not bury them more than 1 in. deep. The yellow flowers sit on the green ruff of the leaves and appear very early in the year, but usually a little after *E. hyemalis* begins to flower.

33

34

35

36

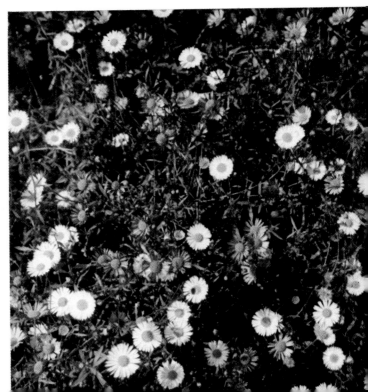

35

Erica carnea (*Ericaceae*) **Mountain Heather**

This plant is a great comfort to those who long to grow heathers but are prevented by soil which contains lime, to which most ericas and all callunas (ling) are averse. It has the additional virtue of flowering in the depth of winter, when flowers are doubly precious. There is a multitude of named forms, varying from those with pure white flowers to others ranging from soft pink to deep red. It has no objection to chalky soil but appreciates liberal amounts of peat if the quantity of lime is extreme. Clip over after flowering and top-dress with humus at least once a year. Propagate by cuttings or by detaching rooted portions.

36

Erigeron mucronatus (*Compositae*)

Admittedly invasive, but one of the most delightful weeds imaginable, and, if confined to crannies in walls, paths or steps, or in sun-baked places in poor soil, never a nuisance. The whole summer through it produces a succession of neat daisy-shaped flowers which are white when they first open, changing quickly to pink and finally to deep rose-red. Never more than 9 to 12 in. tall – dwarfer in really austere conditions – it is a charmer whose faults are easily forgiven. No need to propagate it, it self-seeds freely. *Vittadenis triloba* is a synonym.

37

Erinus alpinus 'Mrs C. Boyle' (*Scrophulariaceae*)

The several varieties of *Erinus alpinus* are so easy to grow and so attractive when they carry their bright flowers in the spring that they should be in every rock garden, and also be permitted to sow themselves into stony chinks and crevices. *E. alpinus* itself carries multitudes of soft lilac flowers on 2 in. stems above neat domes of tiny leaves. There is a form with white flowers, one with deep red blossoms, and the colour of this particular variety is soft, clear pink. Raise them from seed; they may not come entirely true but they are delightful in mixture.

38

Erythronium dens-canis (*Liliaceae*) **Dog's Tooth Violet**

A bulbous plant which flowers in March and April. The bulbs should be planted as early as possible, before summer has become autumn, in cool, moist soil and semi-shade. The leaves are green, handsomely marbled and patterned with colour. The almost cyclamen-like pink flowers are carried on 4 to 6 in. stems. They are to be bought inexpensively as dry bulbs, and they can also be raised from seed but will take some years to reach flowering size.

37

38

39

40

39

Gentiana acaulis (Gentianaceae) **Gentian**

Few will challenge the right of this wonderful plant to be considered the most handsome of a beautiful race. Its huge deep blue trumpets are too well known to need a description. Where it flowers freely they are produced in abundance during the spring, and spasmodically throughout the summer. It likes loam soil and firm planting in an open, sunny place. If it does not flower, move it round the garden until you discover a position of which it approves; a few yards may make all the difference. Propagate by seeds or division.

40

Gentiana septemfida (Gentianaceae) **Gentian**

This really is the gentian for everyman. It has no fads or fancies and will thrive in any good, well-drained soil and in full sun. Its leafy, 9 to 12 in. stems carry clusters of rich blue flowers from mid-summer onwards. It never fails to blossom, and provides plenty of seeds from which young plants can be raised that will flower in the second year. Old plants can be divided, but it is apt to resent root disturbance.

41

Gentiana sino-ornata (Gentianaceae) **Gentian**

Given lime-free soil which is retentive of moisture this is an easy
gentian to grow. It should be planted in March or April as 'thong-roots',
or later in the year from pots, and will flower from mid-August on into
October with large, deep blue trumpet flowers over a green sward of
fine lush foliage. It should be planted in fair-sized groups to make its
best effect, and a lovely picture can be created by planting with it a few
bulbs of *Sternbergia lutea* which gives bright yellow, crocus-like flowers
at the same time as the gentian.

42

Geranium 'Ballerina' *(Geraniaceae)* **Cranesbill**

This is a comparatively new hybrid geranium of great merit. It is the
result of a marriage between *Geranium subcaulescens* and *G. cinereum*,
two valuable rock-garden species. It forms low mounds of divided,
grey-green leaves and begins to flower in May, continuing throughout
the summer to produce a succession of rounded flowers coloured soft
pink and veined with deeper tints. It is seldom out of flower from spring
until autumn. Of rather sprawling habit, each plant should be allowed
a square foot of space in which to develop, and given good, gritty soil
and a sunny position. Propagate by division or cuttings.

41

42

43

44

43

Geum montanum (*Rosaceae*) **Avens**

Not a desirable neighbour for small, choice plants in the rock garden, which it might smother with its fairly large, lobed leaves, but a handsome plant where there is room for its foot-wide clumps. The more than inch-wide, rich golden flowers are beautifully rounded and are carried on 6 to 9 in. stems during the summer. Any good soil pleases it and it is a sun-lover. Propagate it by dividing large plants, or by saving and sowing the seeds after you have enjoyed the spectacle of their tawny, long-awned beauty.

44

Gypsophila fratensis (*Caryophyllaceae*)

A useful trailer to plant so that it can hang from a rocky crevice, or to place between the stones of a sunny wall. It hangs down in a dense curtain of soft grey-green foliage, which changes to clear pink when it is carrying the myriads of small flowers during the spring and early summer. Cut it back with moderate severity after flowering to keep it neat and tidy, and increase it by making cuttings of soft tips in the spring.

45

Hacquetia epipactis (Umbelliferae)

A plant which loves a cool corner in moist, but not saturated soil. It flowers in April and looks curiously like a Winter Aconite (*Eranthis*) for its cluster of tiny yellow flowers is set upon a little green plate formed by its own upper stem leaves. No more than 4 in. tall, it should not be hidden by taller neighbours and its position carefully marked, for it is deciduous and goes to rest early. Propagate by division and seeds.

46

Halimiocistus sahucii (Cistaceae)

This is a bigeneric hybrid between *Cistus salvifolius* and *Halimium umbellatum* and is a valuable dwarf shrub for a really hot, dry situation. About one foot in height, it makes a shapely evergreen bush and is adorned with quantities of large white flowers in clusters of from two to five during June and July. Like all its family it resents disturbance and should never be moved once planted. It is hardy, but appreciates shelter from biting east winds. Propagate it by cuttings made from soft tips early in the year, or harder cuttings of ripened wood with a small heel later on.

45

46

47

48

47

Helianthemum 'The Bride' (*Cistaceae*) **Sun Rose**

Most of the decorative sun roses grown in gardens are forms of *Helianthemum nummularium*. They are unequalled for providing a brilliant show of colour during the summer months. They should be grown in sharply drained soil and sunny positions to be seen at their best but they are tolerant of almost any conditions except shade. Their flowers are of brief duration but are produced in such numbers that there is an almost endless succession. This particular cultivar has white flowers, and other kinds run the gamut from white to glowing wine-red. Increase them by taking cuttings and cut them back after flowering, but do not cut into really hard, old wood.

48

Helichrysum virgineum (*Compositae*)

In very cold gardens and on heavy soil this handsome plant may not be hardy and should be grown in an alpine house. It has strikingly decorative leaves felted with fine silver hairs and heads of buff-pink buds which expand into creamy-white flowers. The blossoms have the papery quality of 'everlastings' and endure for a very long period. It grows about a foot tall, and if grown in a pot should be topdressed or repotted into fresh soil each spring. Propagate from seeds or cuttings.

49

Houstonia caerulea (Rubiaceae) **Bluetts**

A dainty little plant for a cool or half-shaded position in soil which is rich but gritty and does not dry out quickly. Three inch carpets of frail, upright stems clad in tiny light green leaves and surmounted by myriads of little clear blue starry flowers in spring. It roots easily from cuttings, and old plants may be divided in the spring.

50

Hypericum rhodopaeum (Hypericaceae) **St John's Wort**

This is a showy, sun-loving rock-garden plant. Its leaves are soft and hairy and adorn semi-trailing stems which form a low bush, seldom more than 6 in. high. The flowers, borne in mid- to late summer, are soft yellow in colour, and of typical hypericum form with wide-rayed petals and a central cluster of golden stamens. After flowering it benefits from being cut back fairly hard to encourage young growth from the base. Propagate by seeds or cuttings.

51

52

51

Iberis sempervirens 'Snowflake' (*Cruciferae*) **Candytuft**

This perennial, hardy candytuft is almost shrubby in habit, the stiff woody stems rising to a height of about 12 in. It blossoms in the spring in profusion, carrying great quantities of absolutely pure-white flowers in flat heads. If it is planted in very rich soil it tends to grow 'soft' and is then liable to perish during a severe winter. Grow it in gritty soil and full sun and it will endure for many years. Propagate by cuttings of soft tips when these are available. Shoots containing flower buds should never be used as cutting material.

52

Ipheion uniflorum (*Amaryllidaceae*)

This attractive bulb is probably best known under its synonym of *Milla uniflora*, but botanists have now placed it in the genus *Ipheion* (it has also been called Brodiaea and Triteleia). The milk-white or lilac-blue flowers are carried in abundance on 6 in. stems during March and April. Grow it in light soil and plant the bulbs in late summer and early autumn, covering them with about 2 in. of soil. In some gardens it can become a menace, if a beautiful one, as it spreads very rapidly by seeding and by multiplication of the bulbs. It is a sun-lover.

53

Iris reticulata 'Harmony' (*Iridaceae*)

The 'reticulata' irises are among the most popular and beautiful of the early-flowering rock-garden bulbs. They should be planted in August and September, setting the netted bulbs 2 or 3 in. apart and about 2 in. deep in light soil and a sunny position. There are many named varieties, this particular form carrying sky-blue flowers marked with gold on erect, 6 to 9 in. stems. In most gardens these irises will colonize and provide a natural increase.

54

Leontopodium alpinum (*Compositae*) **Edelweiss**

This is a traditional alpine plant, surrounded by myth and legend and often said to be difficult to grow. This is quite untrue as it flourishes in any good soil and an open, sunny position. The tufts of narrow grey leaves are surmounted in early summer by 9 in. stems carrying heads of small flowers surrounded by woolly leaves. The inflorescence has all the appearance of having been made from silver-grey flannel. It can be propagated easily by division or by sowing the seeds, which should be gathered as soon as they can be readily detached from the flower head. They are as light as thistledown and are quickly dispersed by wind.

55

Lewisia howellii (*Portulacaceae*)

Lewisias are sun-loving alpine plants from North America and should be planted in crevices rather than on the flat. They are averse to lime, although they will tolerate it in small amounts. Good drainage is essential and they like to be kept fairly dry after flowering but will take abundant moisture when in full growth. The leathery, glossy, crinkled leaves of *Lewisia howellii* grow in symmetrical rosettes and the numerous flower spikes emerge between the leaves and grow to a height of 9 or 12 in., carrying many salmon-pink flowers. Propagate by sowing the glossy seeds, which will be found to be ready while the capsule is apparently still unripe and green.

56

Linum 'Gemmel's Hybrid' (*Linaceae*) **Flax**

A very decorative, dwarf, yellow-flowered linum of shrubby habit, forming low, compact bushes of rather waxy, grey-green leaves and carrying an abundance of bright golden flowers on erect, 6 to 9 in. stems in early and mid-summer. It likes a hot, dry situation and will grow in any good, sharply drained soil. This is a hybrid which does not form seed and it must be propagated by cuttings made from non-flowering shoots which appear plentifully after flowering.

57

Lithospermum diffusum 'Grace Ward' (*Boraginaceae*)

For many, many years *Lithospermum* 'Heavenly Blue' was a first favourite among rock-garden plants. It has now been replaced by this improved variety, which has slightly larger flowers of equally vivid gentian-blue, and is a better grower. It has an intolerance of lime and, in alkaline soils, should be given generous quantities of peat. It is an evergreen, prostrate-growing shrub, capable of covering a considerable area with its sprawling branches. For many weeks during the summer the entire plant is concealed beneath the countless clear blue flowers. It should be cut back gently after flowering, care being taken not to cut into really old, hard wood. Propagation is by cuttings made from 3 in. soft tips which do not carry flowers. These usually appear in early spring and again after flowering.

58

Lotus corniculatus flore-pleno (*Leguminosae*)

Lotus corniculatus itself is a common British wild plant and, lovely though it is, is too invasive to be trusted in the garden. This form, whose golden and bronze flowers are fully double, is an admirable plant for a hot, dry position in soil which is not very rich. It grows as a prostrate mat of entwined, woody stems and is smothered for long periods during summer with the clusters of handsome flowers. It does not produce seed, and makes a deep tap-root which does not encourage division. Propagation is effected by making cuttings of side-shoots in the spring and summer.

57

58

59

60

59

Mertensia virginica (*Boraginaceae*) **Virginian Cowslip**

A really beautiful plant which was deservedly honoured by receiving the Royal Horticultural Society's Award of Garden Merit. It should be grown in deep, cool, well-enriched soil in light shade or facing north. It is a deciduous plant with a lusty rootstock from which spring leafy erect stems 15 to 18 in. tall and ending in croziers of drooping, bell-shaped, turquoise-blue flowers in spring. The plant dies down quite soon after flowering and its position should be well marked to avoid damage to the fleshy roots during its long dormant period. Propagate it by saving and sowing the seeds, or by careful division of old plants in early spring.

60

Narcissus cyclamineus (*Amaryllidaceae*) **Daffodil**

This is one of the most beautiful of the miniature narcissi which are invaluable for providing very early colour in the rock garden. The small, glossy bulbs should be planted in August and September, spacing them 2 in. apart and covering them with about 1 in. of the light soil in which they like to grow. They can also be naturalized in short grass and open woodland conditions. An excellent example of this can be seen in the Wisley Gardens of the Royal Horticultural Society, where they are plentiful in the wild garden. The rich yellow flowers have a long corona and the perianth segments are abruptly recurved, shaping the flower like that of a cyclamen. It is seldom more than 6 in. in height and flowers in February and March.

61

Nierembergia repens (*Solanaceae*)

From South America and a valuable creeping plant which grows in any good soil but flowers most freely when confined to rather poor, stony, sharply drained soil. It spreads by underground stems which emit leaves to form a green sward on which are poised almost stemless, pure-white, funnel-shaped flowers of considerable size. Propagate by division in spring or autumn. Also known as *Nierembergia rivularis*.

62

Oenothera missouriensis (*Onagraceae*) **Evening Primrose**

A splendid dwarf Evening Primrose for the rock garden, but it must be allowed ample space, for its sprawling, leafy stems will spread over at least 2 square feet of ground when it is in full growth. The immense, rich yellow flowers are produced from shapely, beautifully marked buds and continue throughout the summer. The plant is not more than 1 ft in height and is easy to grow in any good soil and in sun or light shade. Propagate by seeds and by cuttings of soft, non-flowering shoots. Those which appear first from the resting crowns in very early spring make the best cuttings. The plant is sometimes called *Oenothera macrocarpa*.

61

62

63

64

63

Origanum vulgare aureum (*Labiatae*) **Marjoram**

A neat and decorative plant which may have no right to the specific name given here, but by which it is well known and listed in catalogues. It makes tidy mounds, about a foot high—a little more in rich soil—of erect stems clothed with many rounded, rich golden leaves. It is as a foliage plant that it makes its contribution to gardens. Propagate by division in autumn or spring, or by soft-tip cuttings during the summer.

64

Penstemon scouleri (*Scrophulariaceae*)

The dwarf, perennial shrubby penstemons are deservedly popular rock-garden shrublets. This one is most attractive, growing to a height of about 1 ft with innumerable soft lavender tubular flowers during June and July. Many penstemons suffer occasionally from a curious 'die-back' of some of the main branches and a young stock should be maintained to replace any losses due to this trouble. Cuttings made from half-ripened shoots, either cut beneath a leaf joint or taken with a small 'heel' of older wood, root easily and make sturdy young plants. Grow it in full sun and any good soil and preferably in a position not exposed to very cold winds.

65

Phlox subulata 'Benita' (*Polemoniaceae*)

The many named forms of *Phlox subulata* offer a wonderful choice of easily grown and extremely showy plants for the rock garden, for sunny walls, path edges and cracks between paving stones. They all have a prostrate, dense, cushion habit of growth and will flourish in almost any soil which is not waterlogged. They may all be increased by division, by removing rooted layers or by making cuttings of soft growth tips in spring and summer. The particular variety illustrated is a strong grower, capable of covering 2 square feet of ground when fully developed, and covers itself with lavender-blue flowers during the spring.

66

Platycodon grandiflorum mariesii (*Campanulaceae*)
Balloon Bellflower

A deciduous cousin of the campanulas whose erect, leafy stems rise to a height of 15 or 18 in. when in flower. Each stem terminates in a beautiful inflated bud which expands into a huge saucer-shaped deep blue flower in early summer. It likes a sunny position and well-drained soil but is in no way a fussy or difficult plant. Seed is plentifully produced and offers a ready means of increase. For those with very small rock gardens there is a new, very dwarf platycodon named *Platycodon grandiflorum apoyanum* which does not attain more than 9 in. and has similar flowers to those of *P. grandiflorum mariesii*.

65

66

67

68

67

Polygonum vaccinifolium (*Polygonaceae*) **Knotweed**

An invaluable and easily grown, free-flowering rock-garden plant. It is a woody-stemmed evergreen which is ideally placed in a position on top of a wall, or on a high point in the rock garden from which its long stems can depend. The deep pink flowers are produced in great abundance on short, erect spikes from late summer throughout the autumn. It will grow and flower in sun or light shade and is as effective as the pink heather it so much resembles when in blossom. Propagates easily from soft-tip cuttings.

68

Potentilla ambigua (*Rosaceae*)

Probably more correctly named *Potentilla cuneata* but well known under the name given here. It is a tufted plant with woody-based stems holding clusters of short-stalked green leaves which are adorned in June and July by saucer-shaped, inch-wide golden-yellow flowers. For a sunny position in any good soil and does not usually grow higher than 2 to 3 in. Propagate by seeds or division.

69

Potentilla fruticosa farreri (Rosaceae)

There are many cultivated varieties of the shrubby *Potentilla fruticosa*, and they are all valuable garden plants. Many of them are too large for any but a spacious rock garden, but this is one of the less vigorous forms and it is a long-flowering dwarf shrub with many clear yellow flowers carried from early summer until late autumn. Fine green leaves cover slender, erect woody branches and amidst them gleam the golden flowers. Propagate by cuttings. Seedlings can be raised but often produce a miscellany.

70

Potentilla tonguei (Rosaceae)

This is a beautiful hybrid of prostrate habit with sprawling stems which can cover 2 square feet of ground. It should not be grudged the space it occupies, for it produces an abundance of apricot-coloured, crimson-blotched saucer-shaped flowers in the late summer and autumn. It offers a bonus when the foliage adopts rich autumn tints of gold and bronze. A fine carpet for autumn-flowering *Crocus speciosus*. Propagate by division – it does not set fertile seed.

69

70

71

72

71

Primula denticulata (*Primulaceae*)

One of the easiest and most handsome of the bog primulas. Although it loves a genuine bog it will grow very well in an ordinary border or a large pocket low down in the rock garden in any soil which does not parch. Bold tufts of long, narrow leaves emit many tall stems, each carrying a drumstick of flowers which vary in colour according to the particular form from pale purple to carmine-red, and there is a handsome white form. Propagate by root cuttings, division or seed, but the seedlings will vary in colour.

72

Pulmonaria angustifolia 'Mawson's Variety' (*Boraginaceae*)
Lungwort

The lungworts are more usually regarded as wild garden or semi-woodland, or front-of-the-border plants than as being suitable for a rock garden, but there is a place for them in fairly large rock gardens. They have handsome foliage, in some varieties decoratively mottled and splashed with white markings. The plant illustrated is a selected form of *Pulmonaria angustifolia*, long known in gardens, with bold, unmarked leaves and spikes of pink buds which expand into quite large clear blue flowers in the early spring. It will grow in practically any soil or situation other than an arid, sun-baked place. Increase by division of old plants in autumn and spring.

73

Pterocephalus parnassii (Dipsaceae)

To all intents and purposes a dwarf, woolly-leaved scabious with heads of purple flowers on 4 in. stems in the summer. Its carpets of grey foliage are handsome at all times and it is a splendid rock-garden plant of the easiest culture in full sun and any good soil. Propagate by seeds or division.

74

Pyrola rotundifolia (Pyrolaceae) **Wintergreen**

A rare native and not an easy plant unless the ideal conditions are available. It loves to creep by means of white, spaghetti-like roots through sandy, peaty, lime-free soil in shady places. The round, deep-green leathery leaves appear in small clusters and from them rise 9 in. stems carrying several cream-white flowers shaped like those of the lily-of-the-valley. Not easy to propagate, but seedlings can be raised from the dust-fine seed, or rooted plants detached and grown on separately.

73

74

75

Ramonda myconii (Gesneriaceae)

A useful and decorative plant for positions facing north or in semi-shade, ramonda should be planted on its side in vertical or horizontal crevices, positions which it much prefers to a flat bed of soil. In such places the rosettes of dark green, roughly hairy leaves will spread flat against the surrounding stones, and from between the leaves, in May and June, appear the large lavender flowers. In shape the blossoms are very much like those of the potato. In periods of drought ramondas will curl up their leaves, exposing the brown undersides and appearing to be moribund. This is no more than a defence mechanism and the leaves expand again immediately after rain, or a good watering. Propagate by seeds or, with care, by leaf cuttings. It is sometimes known as *Ramonda pyrenaica*.

76

Ranunculus ficaria aurantiaca (Ranunculaceae) **Lesser Celandine**

No one in their proper senses would introduce the common wild *Ranunculus ficaria* into their garden. It is a beautiful but pestiferous weed and almost impossible to eradicate once firmly established. There are, however, several particularly charming forms of the plant which are much better behaved and are sufficiently trustworthy to be cultivated. The best of them is the plant illustrated, which is of neat, tidy habit, forming a cluster of dark green leaves from which, in the early spring, rise short stems carrying large, coppery-orange flowers. It likes rather heavy soil and a sunny position. Propagate by lifting an old plant and separating the small tubers which will be found attached to the roots. These can be grown on into young plants.

77

Rhodohypoxis baurei (*Hypoxidaceae*)

When these plants were introduced from South Africa several years ago they made an immediate appeal with their colourful flowers. They also score heavily with their very long flowering season, for they are in blossom from May until October. They are hardy in many gardens, especially if grown in moist, but well-drained soil. There is but one species, *Rhodohypoxis baurei*, with several forms and now many named varieties. The plant illustrated grows from a fleshy, bulb-like root with a tuft of small, narrow, rather hairy leaves and produces a seemingly endless succession of bright pink flowers composed of a cluster of petals arranged in a rather formless manner. Increase by division and seed.

78

Roscoea humeana (*Zingiberaceae*)

These are deciduous, fleshy-rooted plants which rise late in the spring and often do not make growth until the end of May. The position where they are growing should be carefully marked so that spring planting is not done on top of them. They like deep, moist soil and a cool, semi-shaded position. *Roscoea humeana* grows about 12 in. tall, with long, rather fleshy green leaves, and carries spikes of hooded, violet-purple flowers in July. Propagate by seeds, which must be sought low down in the fleshy flower stem, far below the base of the actual flower.

79

80

79

Saponaria ocymoides (*Caryophyllaceae*) **Soapwort**

A common but valuable rock-garden plant of trailing habit. It should
be planted in a position from which it will hang downwards, forming
a curtain of its long, leafy stems. The bright pink flowers are carried
in great profusion, completely hiding the foliage when the plant is
blossoming during the spring. It is tolerant of most soils and will grow
in sun or light shade. Propagate by cuttings and by seeds.

80

Saxifraga apiculata (*Saxifragaceae*) **Saxifrage**

A very early-flowering saxifrage of the Kabschia section. It grows well
in any gritty soil and a sunny position and will form wide mats of closely
packed green rosettes of tiny, spiny leaves. Above these cushions in
April and May are seen countless heads of lemon-yellow flowers on
4 in. stems. There is a white variety also, which mingles pleasantly with
the type. Propagate by division or cuttings. Like most saxifrages of this
section it appreciates a soil rich in lime, but grows well enough in
neutral soil.

81

Saxifraga longifolia 'Tumbling Waters' (*Saxifragaceae*) **Saxifrage**

Undoubtedly the most magnificent of all saxifrages. The narrow, silver-grey leaves are arranged in very large, completely symmetrical rosettes which are beautiful in themselves. Plant it in a crevice between rocks so that the huge flower spike can hang outwards and arch over in its full grace. Individual flower stems of more than 2 ft in length and a foot in diameter at the base are not unknown, and such an inflorescence will carry many hundreds of the white flowers—a most imposing sight. The rosette which flowers dies afterwards, but side rosettes are usually produced, which may be detached and rooted as cuttings.

82

Saxifraga umbrosa primuloides 'Walter Ingwersen' (*Saxifragaceae*)
London Pride

London Pride, which is the vernacular name for *Saxifraga umbrosa*, is a well-tried garden friend, an inhabitant of many a rough corner where little else would survive, and a very useful ground coverer. This is a miniature form, growing no more than 6 in. tall, with neat rosettes of glossy leaves and dainty deep pink flowers in loose and elegant spikes. It grows well in almost any soil, but has a preference for a cool rather than a hot position. It is a charming associate for such another miniature as the pygmy, golden-flowered *Trollius acaulis*, which is of similar stature and relishes a similar situation.

81

82

83

84

83

Scilla sibirica (Liliaceae) **Squill**

One of the nicest and easiest early spring-flowering bulbs for the rock garden and seen at its lovely best in the form named 'Spring Beauty'. The deep, clear blue flowers are carried in loose clusters on 3 to 4 in. stems. Plant the bulbs in late summer or early autumn, 3 in. apart and 3 in. deep, in well-drained soil and a sunny place.

84

Scilla tubergeniana (Liliaceae) **Squill**

A most beautiful bulb and of comparatively recent introduction but fast becoming a favourite. From the large bulbs spring stems carrying heads of china-blue flowers which are so eager to expand that they begin to open as the stem appears at ground level. As the stems elongate to reach their final 4 to 6 in. the flowers become more abundant. The flowering season is unusually long, and begins with or before the Ides of March. Full sun and light soil.

85

Scutellaria baicalensis (*Labiatae*) **Skullcap**

Although it was introduced from Asia as long ago as 1827, and is an easy plant to grow, this pretty skullcap is all too seldom encountered in gardens. It is a handsome rock-garden plant for late summer flowering, with semi-procumbent stems about 1 ft long clad in glabrous leaves and carrying racemes of hooded purple-blue flowers. Not being fond of too much winter wet, *Scutellaria baicalensis* should be provided with a sunny position in quickly draining soil. It is an excellent plant for a scree large enough to accommodate a plant of its proportions. Propagate by seed or division.

86

Sedum hybridum (*Crassulaceae*) **Stonecrop**

Like many others of its family this sedum spreads rapidly in a sunny position and in almost any soil. It should not be planted too near less-vigorous plants, but is worthy of a position where there is room for it to grow into a low carpet of glossy, evergreen leaves. This is decorated during May and June with bright yellow flowers whose rich colour is accentuated by deep orange stamens. Propagate by division at almost any time.

85

86

87

88

87

Sedum spurium 'Schorbusser Blut' (*Crassulaceae*) **Stonecrop**

In spite of its name a lovely plant asking for no more than a warm, sunny position and any well-drained soil. It makes a close carpet of dark green foliage, which it stains to deep, vivid red when the flowers expand in mid-summer. It makes a magnificent picture when grown together with *Sedum spurium* 'Weihenstephener Gold', which is of similar habit but has golden flowers.

88

Sempervivum marmoreum (*Crassulaceae*) **Houseleek**

Like other houseleeks, this species has been known under many names, including *Sempervivum schlehanii*. It forms dense clumps of medium to large fleshy-leaved rosettes. The leaves are green, with a well-marked brownish tip. The inflorescence is about 9 in. tall and the flowers are crimson, often with a white margin to the petals. Like all houseleeks it loves a hot, dry position and should not be richly fed. Division of the clumps offers a simple method of increase.

89

Shortia uniflora (*Diapensaceae*)

A rare and beautiful plant which demands special care and a well-chosen position. It is a lover of peaty, acid soil and shade and even when provided with ideal conditions, may take a little time to establish after planting. It is an evergreen with rounded, leathery, shining green leaves which take on rich tints of red in the autumn. The spring-borne flowers are large, with delicately fringed petals, coloured soft pink. At no time is the plant more than 9 in. tall. It is intolerant of any conditions other than those suggested above and it would be useless to try and grow it in a sunny rock garden on alkaline soil. Propagation is by seed, which is dust-fine and should be sown, uncovered, on a surface of finely sifted peat or leafmould.

90

Silene schafta (*Caryophyllaceae*)

An old and well-known alpine plant, easy to grow and rewarding in a sunny place in any soil other than heavy clay. It is a tufty perennial up to 6 in. high with innumerable small clusters of rosy-magenta flowers in summer. Propagate it by seeds, or by dividing old plants.

89

90

91

92

91

Tulipa kaufmanniana (*Liliaceae*) **Waterlily Tulip**

The beautiful wild waterlily tulip has been partly submerged beneath
the wealth of splendid hybrids which have been raised during the past
two decades. It is spring-flowering, and the bulbs ought to be in the
ground by early November but earlier planting is advisable if possible.
Set them in a warm, sunny place, 4 or 5 in. apart and 3 in. deep. Wide,
grey-green leaves emerge from the bulbs, and from between them rise
the short stems carrying widely expanded white and yellow flowers of
great beauty.

92

Tulipa batalinii (*Liliaceae*) **Tulip**

This is one of the best of the many lovely dwarf tulip species to grow
in the rock garden. Bulbs should be planted in the autumn, in a warm,
sunny spot. In ideal conditions the bulbs may be left in the ground
for several years, but if there is any doubt as to their winter conditions,
they should be lifted in June, carefully dried and cleaned and stored in
a dry, cool place until it is once more time to entrust them to the soil.
The cream-yellow flowers are carried on 6 to 9 in. stems in the spring.
The petals are pointed and the same colour inside and out but there is
a distinctly deeper yellow blotch at the base of each.

93

Veronica prostrata pygmaea (*Scrophulariaceae*) **Speedwell**

A particularly neat plant, forming little mats of small, dark green leaves and bearing short spikes of intensely blue flowers on 1 in. stems in spring and early summer. There are numerous forms of *Veronica prostrata*, including some with pink and others with white flowers. They all flourish in any good well-drained soil and sun. They may all be propagated by taking cuttings of soft, non-flowering growth tips when these appear. Seed is sometimes set, but seldom produces plants true to type. The plant is sometimes found under the name *Veronica rupestris pygmaea*.

94

Viola cornuta alba (*Violaceae*) **Horned Violet**

A plant which would figure prominently in any list of indispensable plants for the rock garden. It grows easily and well in almost any soil and will enjoy sun or light shade. Its flowering season extends through most of the summer months and, if cut hard back when it seems to be waning, will forthwith make new growth and produce a second abundance of the pure-white flowers which are poised as daintily as butterflies above the light green foliage. It may be increased by cuttings and also from seed, as it comes perfectly true. It is seldom more than 9 in. in height.

93

94

95

96

95

Viola gracilis major (*Violaceae*) **Olympian Violet**

It is reasonably certain that this useful plant has no right to the specific name of *gracilis*. The true *Viola gracilis*, once a plentiful and popular plant in cultivation, is now extremely rare in gardens. The plant illustrated is probably a hybrid with *V. gracilis* somewhere in its ancestry. This need only concern the gardener to whom accuracy of naming is very important. This is an easily grown and very decorative viola with a long flowering period and an abundance of the richly coloured blossoms. Like *V. cornuta alba* it responds well to being cut back periodically. It must be propagated by cuttings or division as it will not come true from seed.

96

Waldsteinia ternata (*Rosaceae*)

A fast-growing, spreading plant, but not depressingly invasive and a most useful carpeter for cool places in any reasonably good and well-drained soil. The glossy, strawberry-shaped leaves are deep green and above them, for many weeks during the summer, are seen loose sprays of bright golden flowers. It is a valuable ground-coverer to use beneath and between shrubs. Propagate by detaching rooted stems or by sowing the seeds. Planted on top of a cool wall it will hang downwards to form a most attractive curtain of pretty leaves and gay flowers. This plant is also known as *Waldsteinia trifolia*.